A Note to Parents and Teachers

DK READERS is a compelling reading programme for
children. The programme is designed in conjunction with

., who
ator
e than
tor

:ographs
a fresh
ADER is
ping his
reading.

ferent
hat

Falkirk Council

you can be sure that you are helping
your child learn to read, then
read to learn!

LONDON, NEW YORK, MUNICH,
MELBOURNE, AND DELHI

Series Editor Deborah Lock
Designer Neetika Vilash
Project Designer Akanksha Gupta
Art Director Martin Wilson
Production Editor Sarah Isle
Jacket Designer Natalie Godwin
Entomology Consultant Professor May Berenbaum,
University of Illinois
at Urbana-Champaign

Reading Consultant
Cliff Moon, M.Ed.

First published in Great Britain by
Dorling Kindersley Limited
80 Strand, London WC2R 0RL

Copyright © 2012 Dorling Kindersley Limited
A Penguin Company

10 9 8 7 6 5 4 3 2 1
001-184581-June 2012

A CIP catalogue record for this book
is available from the British Library

ISBN: 978-1-40938-678-0

Colour reproduction by Colourscan, Singapore
Printed and bound in China by L.Rex Printing Co., Ltd.

The publisher would like to thank the following for their kind
permission to reproduce their photographs:
(Key: a-above; b-below/bottom; c-centre; f-far; l-left; r-right; t-top)

3 **Dreamstime.com:** Adina Chiriliuc (c). **Getty Images:** Andy
Roberts / OJO Images (ca). 4 **Getty Images:** James Porter / Workbook
Stock (t); Sabine Scheckel / Photodisc (c). 5 **Getty Images:** Don
Farrall / Stockbyte (b); James Porter / Workbook Stock (tr). 6-7
Corbis: Ron Wu / Monsoon / Photolibrary. 8 **Getty Images:** Philippe
Mercier / Workbook Stock (clb). 8-9 **Getty Images:** Konrad Wothe /
Minden Pictures. 9 **Getty Images:** Comstock / Comstock Images (t).
10 **Corbis:** Jonn / Johnér Images. **Photolibrary:** imagebroker (br). 11
Dreamstime.com: Andrzej Tokarski (t). **Getty Images:** Paul Tearle /
Stockbyte (bc). 12 **Getty Images:** Stephen Dalton / Minden Pictures.
13 **Getty Images:** Pal Teravagimov Photography / Flickr. 14-15 **Getty
Images:** Paulo De Oliveira / Oxford Scientific. 16-17 **Getty Images:**
Visuals Unlimited, Inc. / Alex Wild. 17 **Getty Images:** Konrad Wothe
/ Minden Pictures (t). 18-19 **Corbis:** Oswald Eckstein. 20 **Corbis:**
Darrell Gulin. 21 **Getty Images:** photoaraki / Flickr (t). 22
Corbis: Anthony Bannister / Gallo Images (t); Fritz Polking / Visuals
Unlimited. 23 **Corbis:** Stephanie Maze (t). 24 **Corbis:** James Hager /
Robert Harding World Imagery (t). 24-25 **Science Photo Library:** Dr
Morley Read. 26 **Photolibrary:** Garry DeLong (b). 27 **Corbis:** Ada
Summer (t). 28 **Getty Images:** Lew Robertson / FoodPix. 29 **Getty
Images:** Gavriel Jecan / Photodisc (t).

All other images © Dorling Kindersley
For further information see: www.dkimages.com

The publisher and author would also like to thank the
entomologists, Dr. Greg Zolnerowich, Gilbert Waldbauer
and Blake Newton for their advice.

Discover more at
www.dk.com

Contents

DK READERS

BEGINNING
1
TO READ

Bugs and Us

Written by Patricia J. Murphy

DK
A Dorling Kindersley Book

Buzz...

Buzz...

Buzz. Buzz.
Swat, swat!
Scratch. Scratch.
Splat, splat!
Insects can
really bug us!

Bugs buzz
in our ears.
Bugs bite or sting us.
Bugs can hurt our crops,
spoil our picnics –
and make people sick!

antenna

head

eye

thorax

"Who needs insects?"
The answer is,
"Everybody does!"

wing

Most insects
do more good
than bad.
Our lives would
not be the same
if there were no bugs.

leg

abdomen

Bees, wasps, flies,
beetles and butterflies
are good pollinators.
They buzz from flower to flower,
spreading pollen.
Pollen helps flowers
to make seeds.

pollen

Some of these seeds

grow into many of the fruits,

vegetables and foods we eat.

Honey bees drink
nectar from flowers
and turn it
into honey.

nectar

They build honeycombs
with beeswax to store
honey and pollen.
Many people and animals
love the taste of honey.
Beeswax is used
to make candles
and other things.

Some insects eat other insects!
This keeps insect numbers
from getting too big.

A praying mantis eating a bee.

Dragonflies eat 300 to 400 mosquitoes in a day. Praying mantises and green lacewings feast on insects, large and small. But, soon, other animals will eat them!

A bee-eater about to catch a dragonfly.

Ladybirds and their larvae
are farmers' friends.
They eat teeny
crop-eating insects
called aphids.

Ladybirds can't get
enough of them!
Many farmers use ladybirds
instead of sprays,
which can harm
other living things.

larva

Some ants protect
plants from harm.
They bite and sting plant-eating
insects and other animals.
They act like bodyguards
for their plant friends.
Other ants move
seeds and soil around
so that new plants can grow.

Ants moving seeds.

Spiders help our gardens to grow,
and keep our houses insect-free.
They catch and collect insects
in their wonderful webs.
These silky, sticky webs are
beautiful to look at.

Many insects are pretty
to watch – and to listen to.
Butterflies flash bright colours
and patterns as they flutter by.
Flickering fireflies
light up the night sky.
Chirping crickets sing
simple songs.

cocoon

Silkworm moths spin cocoons
with silky threads.
People collect the cocoons and
weave the threads together
to make fine silk cloth.
It takes many cocoons
to make silky socks,
dresses and shirts –
and lots of work, too.

Some insects do
nature's dirty work.
Dung beetles eat
the animal dung.

Termites

Termites feed on rotting wood.
Flies and carrion beetles
feed on dead animals.
These insects rid the Earth
of waste – and help to recycle it.

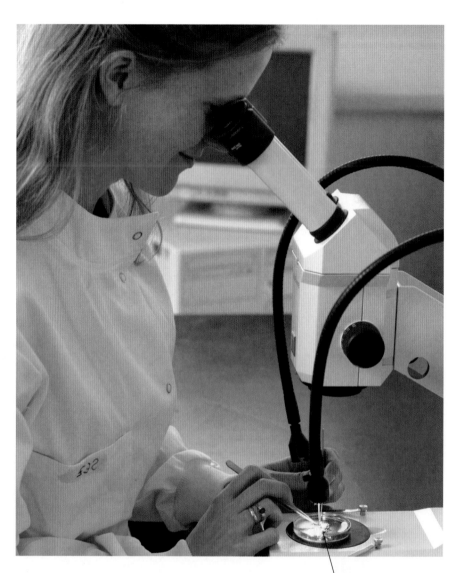

Other insects
help scientists.

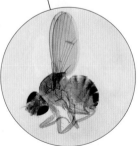

Fruit flies and
flour beetles
show scientists how
animals change
as they grow.

medicine

Mayflies and stoneflies
tell them if streams are clean.
Beetles and butterflies help
them make new medicines
that could save people's lives.

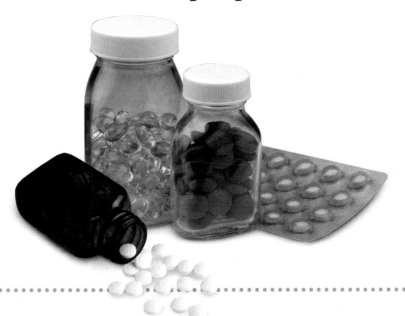

Some people eat insects.

In parts of Africa, people eat
locusts and termites.

In parts of Asia, people cook
beetle larvae and bamboo worms.
These insects are tasty and
good for you – and there are
always plenty around!

Insects help us in many ways.
We can help them, too.
We can plant flowers and
grow plants.
We can learn how to save
their homes.
We can enjoy them –
and let them live.
Buzz.

Buzz.

Buzz.

Buzz.